MW01231440

11 DEADLY PRESENTATION SINS

11 DEADLY PRESENTATION SINS

A Path to Redemption for Public Speakers,
PowerPoint Users and Anyone Who Has to
Get Up and Talk in Front of an Audience

ROB BIESENBACH

Eastlawn Media

Michael: "We'll ask PowerPoint."
Oscar: "Michael, this is a presentation tool."
Michael: "You're a presentation tool!"

—From "The Office"

11 Deadly Presentation Sins

Copyright © 2014 Rob Biesenbach

Published by Eastlawn Media
1339 West Barry Avenue Chicago, IL 60657

ISBN: 978-0-9910814-1-7

CONTENTS

INTRODUCTION:
STUCK IN
POWERPOINT HELL?

It's happening right now. Somewhere in the world, in a windowless conference room or a cavernous ballroom, people just like you are suffering through PowerPoint Hell.

Their only solace is their little smartphone screens, which they use to steal occasional glimpses of an outside world that now seems hopelessly out of reach.

Their tormenter drones on, oblivious to his audience's suffering. His sins are many:

- He fails to take into account their needs and concerns.

- He neglects to tell a compelling story.

- He buries them in information and data without ever giving them a reason to care.

- His visuals are dull.

- His delivery is listless.

In other words, it's business as usual in the corporate world.

Suffering from Death by PowerPoint?

If this sounds depressingly familiar, you're not alone. Researchers estimate that the average office worker, over the course of her career, will spend the equivalent of seven years being subjected to really bad PowerPoint presentations.

That's an exaggeration, of course. It will only *seem* like seven years.

Because the sad fact is, most people are not very good presenters. And maybe—just maybe—you're one of them.

Are You Part of the Problem?

Acknowledging your presentation sins is the first step. Actually doing something about them is the vital second step.

Just the fact that you're checking out this book is a good sign—it means you want to improve.

And that's important. Because few skills are more critical than the ability to present your ideas in clear and compelling terms.

The Power of Presenting

Solid presentation skills can help you in countless ways in business and in life. You'll be better able to:

- Win approval for your projects and budgets
- Close a sale with a customer
- Attract investors

- Motivate employees
- Rally a team
- Ace a job interview
- Earn a raise
- Burnish your reputation
- Spread an idea
- Get out of a speeding ticket
- Run for president of your condo board
- Change the world

And Now for the Good News

The reality is, it won't take much to dazzle people who are accustomed to the usual Bataan Death March that is the average business presentation today.

By adopting just a few of the tips that I give you here, you'll quickly stand out from the crowd of bad presenters.

And if you really devote yourself, you'll be able to deliver the kind of presentations that will make your colleagues run, not walk, to Conference Room B just for the opportunity to see you perform.

And when I say "perform," that's no accident.

Every Communication Is a Performance

About a decade ago, I started a second career as an actor. And I was struck by the parallels between the worlds of performance and business. Both require you to connect with audiences, to tell compelling stories, to express yourself creatively and visually.

All of which just happen to be vital to delivering a good presentation. I believe that every speech and presentation (and every other communication) should be treated as a performance. And if you apply the proven techniques that actors use to make the most of that performance, you're going to be more successful.

In fact, the road to redemption for public speakers runs straight through the world of performance, as you'll learn in the pages ahead.

A Story of Renewal

I've seen for myself the power of presentations to change lives.

In the course of my career, I've written hundreds of speeches for CEOs and other executives for settings ranging from corporate shareholder meetings to national sales conferences to the opening day of Milwaukee's Miller Park ball field.

One of my clients back in the '90s was truck and engine manufacturer Navistar. They were going through a very tough time.

They were getting kicked around by competitors and beaten down by Wall Street, and their employees were in near rebellion. Then a new CEO came on board and vowed to turn the company's fortunes around.

One of the first things we did to help was to organize a three-day meeting for his executive team to present the turnaround strategy to the company's managers.

I wrote a couple of those speeches. (In fact, I had a hand in defining and articulating the actual strategies.) Over three days, the group heard about a new vision for the company, new products in the pipeline, and new ways of doing things.

An Audience Transformed

By the end of the conference, that audience was forever changed.

It was evident in our data: confidence in the company's direction and strategies soared. But more importantly, it showed up in the renewed spirit and outlook of the attendees.

Among their comments:

> "I came here a pessimist and left feeling very positive about our company."

> "I was ready to retire, but now I will get back in the fight to make change happen."

> "I will buy stock!"

For the first time in years, employees felt a real sense of pride in their work and hope for the company's future. It was incredible to witness.

This experience, and others like it, demonstrated to me the power of a great speech—not just to inform but to uplift, inspire, and motivate change.

Redemption Awaits

If you'd like to create and deliver more powerful presentations, this book is a good start. It's filled with practical advice gleaned from years of working with executives, thousands of hours performing onstage, and direct experience delivering speeches and presentations myself.

So if you've been through the fires of PowerPoint Hell, if you've committed any of these deadly presentation sins, you'll find redemption in these pages.

SIN #1:
FAILURE TO UNDERSTAND YOUR AUDIENCE

"The audience is 50 percent of the performance."
Shirley Booth, actor

It's important to understand that this speech is not about you; it's about them—your audience.

And as with most of humanity since time began, the number one question on their collective mind is, "What's in it for me?" So make sure you understand your audience and their needs.

Failure to address their concerns means your speech won't resonate and you'll never get through to them. Punishment for this sin is audience indifference or even outright rejection of your ideas.

Here are six important questions you need to ask before any presentation.

1. Who Are They?

If you're talking to an outside group, find out as much about them as you can. If it's just a few people, as with a sales pitch, Google them and look them up on LinkedIn. If it's a larger audience, get hold of an attendees list.

If they're customers or employees, check out any recent survey data that's available.

Beyond that, talk to the organizer of the event or the person who invited you to speak. What can he tell you about the audience? Ask about their age, experience, interests, and expectations. Go over the other questions listed here.

If you want to go the extra mile, see if you can talk to a few audience members directly. Ask the organizer to hand pick a representative group, and get in touch with them. This is a great way to get an unfiltered read on their concerns.

And you can really make a big impact by referring to these conversations in your speech: "I was talking with Jim from Sales, and he said his number-one concern is making the most of social media."

2. What Do They Want?

It's inevitable that when I sit down with an executive to plan out a speech, the first thing he says is, "This is what I want to tell them" or "This is what they need to know."

Whoa—hold on, cowboy. Before we talk about what *you* want, I want to know what *they* want. And everybody wants something, whether they know it or not.

It might be something tangible, like tools or information or clear direction, or it might be more esoteric things like reassurance or security. Whatever it is, do your research and find out.

Ideally, you want to find that happy intersection where your goals and their needs meet.

3. What's the Context?

Make sure you understand why you were asked to speak at this event. That context is critical to how you frame your remarks.

For instance, you may be told:

  A. We've covered this issue in a lot of detail, but our audience is interested in other perspectives.

  B. They've heard a little about this issue and are dying to know more from an expert.

  C. They don't even know this is an issue—it's not on their radar at all.

Those three scenarios call for vastly different approaches. If you assume they know nothing and they're actually in Scenario A, you're going to end up talking down to them.

And if they're in Scenario C, you're going to have to spend time on the front end educating them on why the issue is important. You'll also have to work extra-hard to scrub your language of jargon and technobabble (which you should be doing anyway).

Next, look at the rest of the program. How many days does this event run? Is there a theme? Who else are they hearing from? Will those people potentially offer alternative perspectives that you might want to address?

At the event itself, drop in on some of the other presentations, roam the hallways, and chat up the other attendees. Absent that, at least check in with the organizers to get a feel for things and understand where your speech fits into the larger puzzle.

Finally, where does your presentation fall on the agenda? First thing in the morning? End of the conference? Before or after lunch? That's going to tell you a lot about your audience's condition and state of mind.

4. What Do You Have in Common?

Think about the things that connect you. If you're talking to employees, it might be pride in the company's heritage. For customers, maybe it's love for the product or brand. For any audience, it might be a mutual frustration (which, by the way, you just happen to have a great solution for).

For a smaller audience—a handful of people—it might be a love of sports or family, a hobby or passion, where you're from, or where you went to school. If you've done your research, you should be able to figure out a few things you have in common.

It's all about finding those cultural or emotional touchstones that bring you together.

5. What Is Their Mood?

These final two questions are not necessarily the most important, but they're probably the most overlooked. First, how are they feeling?

Are they anxious? Frightened? Frustrated? Dejected? Skeptical? Distrustful?

Or are they energized, confident, hopeful, motivated?

Get a read on their mood from the organizers or the audience members themselves. That will shape the tone of what you communicate, which is critical. Because if your speech is tone-deaf, you're never going to get through to them.

6. What Are Their Doubts and Misperceptions?

Finally, find out what they think about you, your ideas, your products or services, and the organization you represent. If they have a negative impression of any of those things, you might have to address it.

Time and again, I've heard clients express fear about "dwelling on the negative." They feel that acknowledging those issues just reinforces them. I believe the opposite: ignoring the negative indicates that you have something to hide.

No, you shouldn't address every little criticism. But for the big things? Be upfront about them. Don't be defensive or make excuses, and certainly don't "dwell." Just acknowledge the issue and move forward.

Like so: "I understand you're frustrated that we haven't made more progress. Believe me, so am I. Here's what we're doing about it."

By acknowledging people's concerns, you show that you're in touch and living in the reality-based world. By ignoring them, you show that you're either clueless or guilty—neither of which is a great option.

A Lesson from Apple

When it comes to communication, Apple has something of a split personality. They can be very closed off and stingy with information, or they can be disarmingly honest and human in their communication.

A few years ago, Apple was having a lot of problems delivering the first white iPhone. It was supposed to come out at the same time as the black iPhone 4. But they ran into some manufacturing problems and had to delay its introduction.

The release date was pushed back a couple of times, and as a result, the company came under a lot of criticism from the technology media and even Apple fans.

So when at long last, almost a year later, Apple introduced the white iPhone, they announced it on their website under the headline, "Finally."

What does this do? If you're an Apple customer, it tells you that the company understands your frustration and is human enough to acknowledge the screw-up. Doing so in a self-deprecating way doesn't hurt, either.

Now this obviously was not a presentation situation, but the same principle applies. Being honest and forthright helps build trust and credibility with your audience.

Know Your Audience

People who fear public speaking often talk in terms of having to "get up in front of a bunch of strangers."

But if you take a few steps to really get to know your audience, and take into account their needs and concerns, they may feel a little less like strangers and more like allies.

SIN #2:
A FLAT OPENING

"We don't know where our first impressions come from or precisely what they mean, so we don't always appreciate their fragility."
Malcolm Gladwell, author

It's been said that when an actor auditions for a role, the casting people make up their minds within the first 30 seconds.

If anything, that's an overestimate.

The sad truth is, when you get up in front of a roomful of people to give your presentation, they are making a thousand little conscious and unconscious judgments about you based on everything from the tone of your voice to the words you use. From the energy you project to the clothes you wear. From the way you walk to whether you remind them of their ex.

So obviously it's important to open strong. And while it's certainly possible to recover from a weak opening, why dig yourself a hole?

What Not to Do

There are lots of ways to open your speech, but first let's talk about what *not* to do. Resist the temptation to begin with any of these tired old standards:

- DO NOT start off in cheerleader mode: "How's everybody doing this morning? What? I can't hear you! I said, HOW'S EVERYBODY DOING THIS MORNING?!" If you try to force the energy like this, you'd better have the personality for it and the goodwill and trust of the audience. Otherwise, you'll just be greeted with groans.

- DO NOT begin with a sales pitch for your company, your product, or your services. I attended a luncheon where the speaker kicked things off by walking us through his book, chapter by chapter. It's fine to sell at some point, but you have to earn that right first by delivering great content.

- DO NOT go into a lengthy recitation of your work or life history. Nobody cares about what you've done until you've given them a good reason to care. Save the details for your program bio, and let whoever is introducing you tee up the highlights. (More on intros later.)

- DO NOT walk us through your agenda right away. Again, give us a reason to care about you and what you have to say first.

- DO NOT break the ice with a hilarious joke you found on the Internet. Everybody's heard the one about the ship and the lighthouse or the Chevy Nova naming disaster. *It means "no go" in Spanish!* (That one's a myth, by the way, but it doesn't stop people from retelling it.) Here's a tip: if you found it online, assume that everyone's heard it already.

- DO NOT start with a dictionary definition. As in, "Webster's defines 'teamwork' as..." I define "clichéd" as attempting this trite, overused tactic that's better suited for a grammar school essay.

If I've just ruined your favorite openers, don't despair. There are plenty of clever ways to start your presentation.

Tell a Story

Nothing beats a well-crafted, well-told story. We are naturally programmed to respond to stories. They put abstract issues in human terms we can relate to. They engage us and make us want to know more.

We'll talk a lot more about stories in chapter 4, but for now the important thing to know is that if you use a story, it should have some relevance to your presentation. A story told just for its own sake is a squandered opportunity.

So if your speech is about teamwork or innovation or change, the story should be about that.

The best thing about storytelling is that it illustrates a problem, and if you've done your homework, it's a problem the audience shares. So right off the bat you're talking about *their* concerns, not yours.

Humanize Yourself

Having said that, not every story has to be "on message." You might want to humanize yourself, giving a glimpse of your character or personality in order to ingratiate yourself with the audience.

That's a fine goal, especially if the audience doesn't know you or maybe has a perception that you want to dispel.

One of the classic story structures is the "Fish Out of Water" tale, sometimes known as "Stranger in a Strange Land." As the titles suggest, it's about being out of your element and the hijinks that inevitably ensue.

This story form works because everyone at some point in their life has felt awkward or out of place, so they will be able to relate to your dilemma. And it's doubly powerful if the waters you describe are those the audience swims in.

I did a speech in Colorado where I opened by playing off of my "flatlander" Midwestern status. Describing a recent ski trip, I noted the surprising difference between a black-diamond slope in Colorado versus those in Wisconsin and showed a stock photo of a dramatic wipeout.

They ate it up. They appreciated the show of humility, my willingness to "try their waters," and the acknowledgment that theirs were maybe better.

So think about an awkward moment you've had that can be used to gain your audience's empathy and appreciation.

Relate an Everyday Event

The simplest, easiest story to tell begins with the old, "A funny thing happened on my way to the conference..." Everybody can relate to traffic jams or baggage mishaps or those tiny hotel soaps.

It's like the old "Seinfeld" episode where George and Jerry pitch their "show within a show" to NBC:

> GEORGE: "What'd you do today?"
>
> RUSSELL: "I got up and came to work."
>
> GEORGE: "There's a show. That's a show."
>
> RUSSELL: "How is that a show?"

A little story about nothing can have a surprisingly big impact. You woke up in your hotel room not knowing what city you were in. You accidentally set your alarm to PM instead of AM. Your in-flight magazine came with the crossword puzzle already filled in.

These are the small life moments that everyone has experienced. They won't provoke fits of laughter, but they will trigger knowing nods and glimmers of recognition. And that will help people relate to you.

Now if you can find a way to make this little anecdote underscore the point of your speech, all the better.

Ask a Question

Starting with a question works on several levels. It gets the audience involved early. It shows that you care what they think. And it signals that the presentation is not going to be just about you.

When I'm presenting on the subject of presentation skills, I'll often start by asking the audience to think of a great speech they've seen, and then together we make a list of the qualities that made those speeches so powerful and memorable.

Now if I've done my job, I've anticipated most of what they'll say (compelling visuals, passion, interaction, energy, etc.) and will have that covered in the presentation, making me look like some kind of clairvoyant super-genius.

And for those things I haven't anticipated, I can take a moment here and there to address them, making me appear super-sensitive and responsive to the audience's concerns.

So think about a question to tee up your content. Just be aware of the old lawyers' axiom: "Never ask a question you don't know the answer to." If you get responses that completely undermine what you're prepared to say, you're going to start off on shaky ground.

Take a Poll

If you have access to one of those automated polling systems, think about how you can use it. People love to weigh in with their opinion—it makes them feel their thoughts are valued.

Of course, you can take a poll in traditional analog mode as well: "With a show of hands, tell me what you think is the most important element of a speech: content or delivery technique?"

You could even use the poll as a launching point for a quick conversation: "For those who answered 'delivery technique,' does anyone want to tell me why you think that's most important?" After that, you can solicit an opposing view.

Just be careful. You need to control the conversation so that it doesn't devolve into chaos. But if you do it right, you set a really positive tone, and you get people involved early by giving them a stake in the outcome.

Wait, There's More!

Here are a few other ways to kick things off:

- Use a quote from a literary figure, sports legend, business expert, or other authority. Just try to find one that's not overused.

- Cite a study, a statistic, or research that underscores your point. Don't get too hung up on numbers, though—keep it simple: "Studies show that people's number-one fear is public speaking."

- Make an audacious claim: "Most people are terrible presenters."

If you're still stumped, professional speaker and trainer Patricia Fripp (who happens to be the sister of guitar great Robert Fripp—think David Bowie's "Heroes") has a great list of opening lines. A few of my favorites:

- "How often have you experienced..."

- "It was the scariest moment of my life..."

- "Like you, I was brought up to believe..."

Plan Your Introduction

Your speech begins before you step up to the podium. People will look at your bio in the program, Google you, maybe even go to your website. And if you're at a more formal setting, such as a conference, you'll probably be introduced by someone.

This is why you don't have to recite your full bio at the beginning of your speech. Let these other sources speak for you so that you can get down to the business of your remarks.

As with every other element of your speech, you'll want to try to control the intro as much as possible. It's a good idea to prepare your own and give it to the organizers. Otherwise, they may cobble together something based on information that's inaccurate or irrelevant to your content.

I have several intros I use, depending on the subject of the speech. Here's one for presentation skills:

> Rob Biesenbach is a corporate communications expert, actor, and author. He's written hundreds of speeches for CEOs and other executives and is a professional speaker himself. He's a former VP at Ogilvy PR and press secretary to a state attorney general, among other things. A Second City–trained actor and improviser, Rob has appeared in more than 150 stage and commercial productions in the past decade. He brings these two worlds together in his books, *Act Like You Mean Business* and *11 Deadly Presentation Sins*.

Of course, I'm always happy if they want to craft their own intro, but this at least gives them something to go on. The main thing, other than hitting the key points, is for the intro to be short. As a general rule, your intro should not be longer than your speech. Under a minute will do, unless you're a head of state or something.

Other elements of your background can go into the program bio or be revealed more organically as you speak: "Here's a lesson I learned from working for a nonprofit..."

One final note on intros: if you have a difficult name like mine, provide a pronunciation key, as in "Rob Biesenbach (BEE-sen-bock)."

Hit the Ground Running

Obviously, how you *perform* your opening remarks is just as important as how well you craft them. To preview some of the points in coming chapters: you'll want to clear your head, focus your thoughts, stand up straight, walk confidently, and pump up the energy and volume.

And, of course, practice, practice, practice until you get your opening just right. It would be a sin to waste this opportunity to make a strong first impression.

Resources

- *Patricia Fripp's Opening Options ... the Words*, by Patricia Fripp

SIN #3:
LACK OF FOCUS

"When you're telling these stories, have a point.
It makes it so much more interesting for the listener."
Steve Martin, *Planes, Trains and Automobiles*

Bad speakers tend to ramble on and on. And on.

And for millennia, they were allowed to indulge their chatty nature within the luxurious format of a two- or three-hour stem-winder. Without TV or the Internet, what else were audiences to do?

But time limits on speeches are being driven ever downward. The 60-minute speech is becoming a relic as quaint as the roomy seat in coach. Even 40 minutes is pushing it.

TED Talks are among the world's most celebrated speeches, and they have an 18-minute limit. Go online and you'll find that many experts are recommending a 20-minute cap on keynotes.

Communications coach Carmine Gallo calls it the "Goldilocks Zone"—neither too short nor too long, but just right—and cites brain research suggesting that "cognitive backlog" occurs when too much information is piled on.

Of course, there is no one-size-fits-all standard. A how-to training session is going to be different from a featured dinner speech.

But for the most part, it's becoming more and more important to focus your thoughts and err on the short side—particularly in a world where attention deficit is less a disorder than a feature.

So what can you do to avoid the sin of rambling and pare down your presentation to the essentials? Here are a few tips.

No Speech Is an Island

Understand that this presentation is just one opportunity among many to get your message across. What you say can be supplemented before, during, and after the speech, with handouts, workbooks, leave-behinds, links to web pages, videos, follow-up emails, and many other things.

So your job is to figure out what exactly needs to be conveyed here that can't be communicated just as well or better in any of those other ways.

Think about what makes a speech special:

- People can watch you live, in person, and in three dimensions.

- You can more easily convey warmth, emotion, and passion.

- Audience interaction is more fluid.

- Audience participation and exercises are easier to accomplish.

- You can harness and feed off the energy in the room.

- You can better gauge audience reaction, seeing it for yourself in people's expressions and body language, and making adjustments as necessary.

All of that is vastly different from what you can accomplish in a memo, an online chat, or even a Skype session or Google Hangout.

How can you put all those advantages to work for you? You can start by focusing less on information and more on inspiration. Less on lecture and more on conversation.

For every element of your presentation, ask yourself, "Why here? Why now? Is there a better way or a better time to communicate this information?"

That's a good general starting point. Here are a few other ways to narrow your content.

Know, Feel, Do

This is a classic construction that I have had great success with. Start with the basics.

What Do You Want Your Audience to Know?

That's the information, the data—the easy stuff, really. Sadly, many presentations start and end right here.

But merely passing along information is the very least you

can accomplish with a presentation. And if that's all you're doing, you might as well just send the audience a memo. You've got these people in a room together—don't squander that opportunity. Make your presentation about something more.

Which brings us to the next phase...

What Do You Want Them to Feel?

Emotion is a critical driver of people's decision-making. It's been said that people buy on emotion and justify with logic.

And countless studies have shown that you can throw all the facts you want at people, but you're not going to change their minds unless you win their hearts.

So you want them to feel something: motivated, inspired, reassured, challenged, chastened, frightened. That's the trigger that gets us to the next phase.

What Do You Want Them to Do?

Do you want them to implement your idea? Approve your project? Grant your budget? Buy your product? Join your cause? Seek more information? Check out your website? Invite you to the next round?

Whatever action you want them to take, make it clear, and let that serve as a filter for the information you choose to include in and omit from your speech.

Three Takeaways

I do a presentation on storytelling in which I outline a three-part structure for stories. (More on this in the next chapter.) An audience member once told me that he went to a seminar that taught eight ingredients for stories. He couldn't recall any of them. But he felt confident that he could work with three.

That's just the way the brain works. We can grasp only a handful of ideas at a time—about three to five.

So take a look at your content and think about the three most important things for your audience to know. Make your speech about those three things.

Now what if you have a 14-Point Plan to Change the World? You could make it a five-point plan instead. Or you could group the points into three categories.

Or you could prioritize, spending the majority of your time on the three most important points, and then just list the rest. (Remember, you have other ways to get that additional information to them—a website, a whitepaper, a book, etc.)

One Walkaway

The three takeaways are a great way to narrow down your laundry list of information—the specs, the features, the benefits. The stuff.

In terms of how you want them to *feel*, a great question to ask is, "What do I want them to walk out of the room saying?" Here are some possibilities:

- "Wow, I had my doubts, but now I'm convinced."

- "This sounds like a really cool idea. I want to find out more."

- "I am so fired up about the company's future."

- "This guy is a great leader/innovator/strategist/ futurist/etc."

- "This is someone we can trust."

All of this, of course, should closely tie in with your audience's needs and interests, which you should have a good handle on if you've gone through the recommendations in chapter 1.

How Do You Stand Apart?

So you've presented your ideas. Chances are, lots of other people and businesses have similar ideas. Why are yours better?

Make sure you take some time to differentiate yourself. Because if you manage to convince the audience that they need whatever solution you're selling (literally or figuratively), you want to make sure they "buy" from you and not a competitor.

How do you stand out? Skills? Experience? Cost, value, responsiveness, speed, enthusiasm, friendliness, results, ratings, reviews?

Think about what sets you, your idea, your product or service apart from the crowd.

One Possible Template

Since there are so many different types of speeches and presentations, a single one-size-fits-all template for your content is hard to come by. But if I had my back to the wall, here's an outline I would recommend:

- Define the problem/opportunity.
- Propose a solution.
  - Point 1
  - Point 2
  - Point 3
- Explain why your solution is better.
- Close the "sale"—ask for something.

The great thing about this structure is that it starts by putting you in your audience's shoes. You are talking about the thing that matters most to them: themselves.

How It Plays Out

Here's how you can apply this template for three different types of speeches.

Step	Scenario A: Appeal to Employees
Define the Problem/ Opportunity	I know many of you are worried about our performance.
Propose a Solution	Our new strategy is aimed at boosting earnings in the coming year.
Three Key Points	We're pursuing cost savings, strategic investments, and new technology.
Why It's Better	This is the recommendation of a six-month, exhaustive study by outside experts who have successfully turned other companies' fortunes around.
Call to Action	To make these changes happen, we're asking you to offer recommendations for how your department will meet these goals.

Scenario B: Sell a Product	Scenario C: Pitch an Idea
Like most people, you're probably worried about whether you'll have enough money to retire on.	Traffic congestion and pollution are major problems affecting quality of life for city dwellers.
This system will help you calculate exactly how much you need to retire and make sure you stay on plan.	Many cities are having great success with bike-sharing programs.
It takes an hour to set up, it automatically updates, and it sends you reminders when you're falling short of your goals.	Bike sharing offers commuters affordability and convenience and takes auto traffic off the streets.
This system offers more options and flexibility than free versions on the market but costs a fraction of what you'd pay a financial planner.	This vendor has a strong track record of service in other communities and provides 24-hour fleet management and service.
You can try it for free for 30 days.	We'd like to do a pilot in three neighborhoods to show you how it works.

Leave Them Wanting More

Understand that if you try to say everything, you'll end up communicating nothing. So keep it focused.

With a short presentation especially, your goal should be to call your audience's attention to an issue or problem, suggest a solution, hit a few key points, and get them intrigued enough to want to know more.

Remember: every time a speaker finishes early, an angel earns its wings.

Resources

- "Why a 20-Minute Presentation Always Beats a 60-Minute One," by Carmine Gallo, *Forbes*

SIN #4:
BAD STORYTELLING

"How do you communicate to 38 million people? It's the narrative, the drama. Who's the protagonist? Who's the antagonist?"
Jerry Brown, Governor of California

Storytelling is one of the most powerful forms of communication there is. If you want to make an impact, if you want your points to stick, nothing beats a well-told story.

Stories lend context and meaning to your ideas. They lift people up and inspire them. They elevate your presentations to a higher plane.

Some people are intimidated by the idea of storytelling. They think it's a special skill reserved for novelists or songwriters or those folksy cowboys telling tall tales around the campfire.

Others tend to overestimate their storytelling abilities. They're accustomed to passing off mere happenings and anecdotes as full-fledged stories.

The truth lies somewhere in between. I believe anybody can tell a story. But there are a few important guidelines to follow that will give your stories greater impact.

Before we get into that, let's talk about why storytelling is so effective.

Why Stories Are So Powerful

All our lives we're immersed in stories. We're raised on them—bedtime stories, fairy tales, cartoons. And we are continuously bombarded by stories, courtesy of the vast entertainment and media complex.

Americans spend $10 billion a year going to the movies, $15 billion on video games, and 35 hours a week watching TV. So storytelling structure is ingrained in our consciousness.

But it goes even deeper than that. Our brains are actually hardwired for stories, a result of 100,000 years of human evolution that has required us to process the events around us and communicate our ideas and beliefs to others.

In fact, one study showed that when we hear a story, it stimulates the same area of the brain that is activated when we experience an event. Think about that: as far as the brain is concerned, story and experience are pretty much one and the same. And experience is one of the most important ways we learn.

If you're not convinced, just Google the subject and you'll find study after study, article after article, attesting to the unique power of stories to shape opinions and influence people.

We inevitably respond to the familiar rhythms and patterns of stories. And that's why story structure is so important. If you don't get the structure right, you'll defy your audience's expectations and diminish your impact.

What Is a Story?

So what exactly is a story? There are lots of definitions out there. Marketing executive Jim Signorelli found 82 different definitions when he was researching his book, *StoryBranding*.

The one he finally settled on is similar to what I was taught at Chicago's famed Second City training center. A story consists of three critical elements:

> A **character** in pursuit of a **goal** in the face of an **obstacle** or challenge.

How the character resolves (or fails to resolve) the challenge creates the dramatic tension that keeps us tuned in.

There are undoubtedly other elements to a story—a surprising twist, a moral lesson—but these are the three essential building blocks. Omit any one of them, and what you end up with is less a story than an anecdote. *If that.*

Spotting Stories in the Wild

The best way to learn how to tell stories is to study this structure in action. So let's look at a few examples from popular culture:

- Take one of the classics of Western literature, *Romeo and Juliet.* Our main characters are a pair of naïve young lovers. Their goal is to be together. The challenge, or obstacle, is the blood feud that divides their families. Romeo and Juliet are ultimately thwarted in their goal (in this life, anyway).

- Or look at the movie *The Fugitive*. The main character is Dr. Richard Kimble, a man who's wrongly accused of killing his wife. His goal is to prove his innocence. The obstacle is the federal marshal sworn to bring him to justice. That conflict helps keep us on the edge of our seat.

- From the world of television, there's the quintessential sitcom "I Love Lucy." Our character is a zany redhead married to a bandleader. Her goal (in practically every episode) is to break into show business. Her obstacles vary from week to week and include her husband Ricky's objections, Lucy's delusions about her talent, and her tendency to squander opportunities by overreaching. Hilarity, as they say, ensues.

Think about your favorite movies and TV shows and see if you can identify this simple formula at work. The more you study it, the better you'll be able to put it to use in your presentations.

Find Your Own Stories

You can go online and find lots of stories about historical figures overcoming great challenges. But chances are, your audience has already heard them. It's better to create your own.

I believe that every person, every organization, has a vast reserve of untold stories just waiting to be found, shaped, and shared. So in preparing your presentation, think about your audience's challenges, and ask these questions:

- What are the top concerns or issues they're dealing with?

- Can you think of an occasion when you've faced a similar challenge? How did you overcome it?

- Or is there someone within your organization, among your customers, or in your community who can serve as your main character? An everyday hero blasting through obstacles and achieving her goals?

- Is the hero right there in your audience? If you've done your research, you can uncover those stories.

Of course, the better the character, the better the story. Your characters should be relatable. After all, why do we still watch Lucy over a half-century later? Because we *love* her—or at least we identify with her.

The beauty of the story approach is that you are speaking directly to your audience's concerns. So use stories often and early.

Example: Estela and the Candy Factory

Here's one of my favorite stories, taken from my client experience. A company that manufactures candy and gum wanted to demonstrate its commitment to quality and safety. So we went looking for stories.

I was on the plant floor talking with a worker named Estela. I asked her what she did to ensure quality, and she walked me through her processes and showed me her checklists and demonstrated how the machines worked. It was impressive, but it didn't really grab me.

So I asked about her family, and she totally lit up. "They

call me the Candy Lady," she beamed. She pointed to a code on one of the packages that indicates when and where the product was made.

Here's the kicker: her kids can read the code. So whenever they go to the store, they run to the candy aisle, turn over the packages, and say, "This is Mommy's gum! My mommy made this gum." The bottom line: it's good enough for your family because Estela is there every day making sure it's good enough for hers.

Now *that's* a story. It's got a **character** at its center whom we can relate to—a mom. Her **goal** is to produce a quality product. Her **challenge** is to stay focused while performing the same task eight hours a day, five days a week. She resolves that challenge by treating her customers like family.

Unleash the Power of Stories

I've told the story of Estela and the candy factory many, many times, and it never fails to create an intense, visceral reaction from audiences. They lean in, they nod, they smile, they audibly go, "Awwww." I get choked up myself telling it.

Here's what makes this and other stories so powerful:

- Stories put a human face on an issue. The truth is, nobody cares about programs or processes—they care about people.

- They connect us. You don't have to be familiar with the manufacturing world or quality-control measures to get this story, because it's really about a mother's love for her children and her desire to keep them safe.

- Stories humanize us. Especially when we tell a story about ourselves, it gives people a glimpse into who we are and what we stand for. It makes us more relatable.

- They raise the stakes. No longer is this about data or processes—it's about family, love, pride, safety, and health. Stories take us out of the everyday and remind us of the larger world, the universal truths.

- Finally, great stories appeal to us on an emotional level. And emotion carries special power to move and convince people.

In fact, emotion is so important, it just happens to be the subject of its own chapter, coming up next.

Resources

- "Your Brain on Fiction," by Annie Murphy Paul, *New York Times*

- "The Science of Storytelling: Why Telling a Story Is the Most Powerful Way to Activate Our Brains," by Leo Widrich, *Lifehacker*

SIN #5:
NO EMOTIONAL PULL

"The market is not seduced by logic. People are moved by stories and drama and hints and clues and discovery. Logic is a battering ram."
Seth Godin, marketing expert and author

This is a difficult concept for many left-brained people to grasp, but facts and logic are rarely the best way to convince an audience.

There's a reason why facts are described as cold and hard: they don't have the power to warm hearts, which is the key to changing minds.

So instead of burying us in information and data, give us a reason to care. Make us *feel* something. Invest your arguments with emotion, and you'll transcend our earthly objections.

Emotion and the Brain

As with story, emotion goes to work on our brains in a unique and powerful way. Here's how molecular biologist John Medina describes it in his book, *Brain Rules*:

> An emotionally charged event ... is the best-

processed kind of external stimulus ever measured. Emotionally charged events persist much longer in our memories and are recalled with greater accuracy than neutral memories.

In another influential book, *Made to Stick: Why Some Ideas Survive and Others Die*, authors Chip and Dan Heath argue that emotion is one of the key factors behind why some ideas catch fire and others don't.

In fact, the person who popularized the "stickiness" effect, Malcolm Gladwell, has had incredible success using stories and emotion to make the findings of sociologists and researchers accessible to everyday readers.

I once had the pleasure of watching Gladwell give a dinner speech. Using no notes or visuals, he managed to keep a thousand people spellbound through masterful use of story, character, and emotion.

Emotion Humanizes You

So, yes, there's plenty of science behind the power of emotion. But to me, the most authoritative argument comes, as it usually does, from "Star Trek." (The original series, of course.)

As we all know, Mr. Spock is ruled by logic. But in the episode "Amok Time," he's afflicted with a nasty bout of Pon Farr (sort of the Vulcan equivalent of spawning season). In a hormone-fueled frenzy, he hijacks the *Enterprise* and takes it to his home planet, where he kills his captain and best friend, James T. Kirk.

Or so he thinks. After dutifully turning himself in for court martial and a sure death sentence, Spock is shocked to discover his old friend alive and well. He wheels about, grabs Kirk by the shoulders, and with a great, human grin on his face, cries out, "Jim!"

It's this spontaneous outpouring of emotion that forever endears audiences to Spock. He gives us what we all crave—that tiny glimpse of humanity.

A proper display of emotion helps humanize you. It inspires empathy, creates common ground, and breaks down the walls between you and the people you're trying to reach.

Audiences will forgive a multitude of presentation sins for speakers who open themselves up and show their humanity.

Lower Your Deflector Shields

I've worked with many executives who are reluctant to show emotion. Some say they don't think audience members—employees particularly—want to see that personal side. Others admit that they're just not comfortable showing the cracks in the façade.

If this is you, I respectfully urge you to get over it. Revealing a bit of who you are—your humanity—is a basic element of leadership. Much has been written about the importance of "authenticity" in leaders. I consider emotion and storytelling the best routes to showcasing your authentic, true self.

So get fired up, get choked up, get a little righteously indignant now and then. Few things are more powerful than emotion for breaking through to resistant audiences and winning them over.

Drill, Baby, Drill

But let's say you're the stoic type—more Spock than Kirk—and free-flowing emotion doesn't come naturally to you. No worries. Allow me to switch metaphors.

I talk about "tapping into" emotion because it's a little like drilling for oil. I believe everyone has vast emotional reserves somewhere within.

For some people, those reserves lie just below the surface and are easy to access. For others, the emotion is buried deep, and you have to resort to drastic measures. The equivalent of hydraulic fracking, if you will.

So how do you tap into that emotion so you can be more persuasive in your speeches and presentations? I recommend three levels of exploration, starting near the surface and drilling deeper with each phase.

These steps can be applied in a variety of situations, from rallying a group of employees to soothing nervous investors to winning over customers.

Level 1: Career

It's important to show people not just *what* you do but *why* you do it. So think about answers to these questions:

- What do you love about your job?

- What makes you jump out of bed in the morning?

- How does your work contribute to the big picture?

- How does your organization/product/service make people's lives better, in ways big and small?

- Are you proud of what you do? Why?

- What about the company's history and heritage—are you proud to be part of that?

One thing I've found in all my years in business is that most people, from C-suite executives to workers on the production line, take pride in what they do. They want to feel that their work matters and that they're contributing to something bigger than themselves.

But if none of this gets your emotions flowing, proceed to the next level.

Level 2: Outside Passions

Do you have a hobby or interest outside the workplace that keeps you occupied? Do you paint, sculpt, craft? Do you play golf, tennis, softball, bridge? Are you a singer, guitarist, pianist, karaoke singer?

Whatever it is, think about how and why it brings you joy or satisfaction. Is it the opportunity for self-expression? The endorphin rush? The discipline, the focus, the drive it takes to master a skill?

Now, how can you relate those feelings back to the larger point you're making? "You know, when I'm standing in front of a blank canvas, it gets me excited, because I see endless possibilities..."

If your well remains dry, it's time to go deeper.

Level 3: Personal Life

Almost everyone has had a mom or dad, a spouse or significant other. Many have brothers, sisters, children, nieces, nephews, or cousins.

Assuming these people are important to you, think about these things:

- What do you love about them?

- What makes them special?

- How did they make you who you are?

- What's the best lesson your dad or mom taught you?

- What do your kids think you do?

- Do you get to spend as much time with your family as you'd like?

- What sacrifices have you made for your career? Missed birthdays, recitals, etc.

- What do you miss most when you're away from your family?

Getting this personal won't be right for every group or occasion, of course. And you will need to connect this discussion to the substantive point you're trying to make. But talking about those who are closest to you is an important way to draw others closer.

Can You Go Too Far?

When I'm presenting this material to audiences, someone inevitably asks, "How much is too much?" As marketing strategist Dorie Clark puts it, there's a fine line between emotional availability and TMI.

If you have trouble establishing that line, let's start with the obvious. You should not put your fist through a wall or break furniture. You shouldn't cry hysterically and uncontrollably. You shouldn't choke up every time you talk about loyalty or teamwork.

Much of this comes down to the ability to exercise normal human judgment and read the visual and emotional cues of others.

One thing they teach us in acting is that fighting back tears and just managing to control them is far more powerful than openly weeping. Think about George W. Bush in the Oval Office after September 11. Think about Barack Obama when he discusses a tragedy involving children and how it reminds him of his own daughters.

A good guideline is the old "Less is more."

Are the Rules Different for Women?

This is the second most common question I get on the subject of emotion. And I admit to feeling somewhat handicapped by the fact that I'm a man.

But I do pose this question to powerful, successful women I know, and what I've found is ... it all depends. Every person, every culture, is different.

I have a client who's a plant manager in a small town. It's a very unusual job for a woman, and she's faced her share of backward thinking. She says that if she tried the "pound-on-the-table" style of indignation, it would feed right into some of the worst stereotypes about women.

Another woman who's a high-powered consultant detects a lot of passive-aggressive judgment from her mostly male colleagues, which causes her to often temper how she expresses herself.

From what I've observed, the emotional spectrum a woman can operate in is probably narrower than that for a man. So be wary of the extremes. Also, keep in mind that positive displays of emotion—passion, pride, enthusiasm, love—are a lot less likely to backfire.

Live Long and Prosper

One final note, just in case it's not clear. When I talk about emotion, I don't mean uncontrolled outbursts in reaction to a crisis or conflict. I mean the judicious use of emotion, applied strategically and for a purpose. Not contrived, of course. Just channeled.

If that makes you uncomfortable, you need to work on it. If you're a leader, especially, people want to see that side of you. They crave that human connection.

Emotion is too powerful a tool to keep it bottled up all the time.

Resources

- "Your Brain Lies to You," by Sam Wang and Sandra Aamodt, *New York Times*

- "What's the Line Between Authenticity and TMI?" by Dorie Clark, *Forbes*

SIN #6:
DULL, UGLY VISUALS

"Image is our first choice, dialogue the regretful second choice."
Robert McKee, *Story*

Here's one that really baffles me. We've all heard that a picture is worth a thousand words. We've seen TED Talks where the speakers are accompanied only by big, beautiful images.

And we watched Steve Jobs mesmerize audiences with elegant, visually stunning presentations.

Yet so many people still don't get it. Here's how former Jobs protégé and marketing superstar Guy Kawasaki put it:

> Take a look at Steve's slides. The font is sixty points. There's usually one big screenshot or graphic. Look at other tech speakers' slides— even the ones who have seen Steve in action. The font is eight points, and there are no graphics. So many people say that Steve was the world's greatest product introduction guy ... don't you wonder why more people don't copy his style?

Why Do Most Presentations Stink?

I do wonder. I think some people are accustomed to using their slides as a script, which is a really bad idea. Remember, it's called *visual* support. As a colleague likes to say, "'Insert Text Here' is a suggestion, not a command."

Others probably don't want to take the time to make their presentation more visually appealing. And it can take a lot of time, especially if you do what many experts suggest: toss out your PowerPoint template and create your presentation from scratch.

Still others probably believe that what they're saying is so fascinating, it doesn't require any fancy visual support. Or their ideas are so complex, they can't possibly be reduced to simple graphics.

All of them are wrong. A special circle in hell is reserved for speakers who persist in inflicting dense, wordy slides on audiences.

Why Visuals Are So Powerful

There's an important scientific principle called the Picture Superiority Effect. Here's how presentation expert Marta Kagan explains it in an excellent post on Hubspot:

> [H]umans more easily learn and recall information that is presented as pictures than when the same information is presented in words. In one experiment, for instance, subjects who were presented with information orally could remember about 10% of the content 72

hours later. Those who were presented with information in picture format were able to recall 65% of the content.

So in terms of stickiness, images are at least six times more powerful than words.

But we know this, right? We were raised on "show and tell" in school. We consume thousands of hours of television and movies every year, where the concept of "Show, don't tell" reigns.

It's why playwright and screenwriter David Mamet urges TV writers to "pretend the characters can't speak, and write a silent movie." He knows that words are just one way—often the least effective way—to get our point across. And that TV and movies are a visual medium.

I would argue that *life* is also a visual medium.

So use more pictures in your presentations. Not only is it a more effective way to get your ideas across; it's also far more interesting for your audience.

Go for Quality

Of course, you don't have to use slides at all—some speakers get along just fine without them. But if you do, make sure they're good.

Don't settle for just any old pictures. Certainly not tired old clip art. You want to use compelling images, full of power and impact.

Seth Godin wrote a great treatise called "Really Bad

PowerPoint," in which he said:

> Talking about pollution in Houston? Instead of giving me four bullet points of EPA data, why not read the stats but show me a picture of a bunch of dead birds, some smog, and even a diseased lung?

Not every audience is going to want to see a dead bird (especially at a luncheon address), but they will appreciate and pay attention to images that break the mold.

Where to Find Great Pictures

So where do you find powerful, original images to illustrate your content? Here are some ideas.

Don't Steal Images

First, here's what *not* to do. Don't just do a Google Image search and pull pictures down from there. Those images belong to other people, and by the time they show up in your search results, the identity of their original creators is long since lost to the ages.

And it's wrong to use other people's creative work without permission. Sure, you could probably get away with it in an internal setting, where you're presenting to a few people around the office. It's still not right, but you probably won't get in trouble.

But when you start to do public speeches, especially ones with commercial intent, you need to be more careful. That means if you're being paid to speak or you're selling something, either directly (*Buy my book!*) or indirectly (*Think of my company for this service*), you should use rights-managed images.

Pay for Stock Photography

Stock photography sites like iStockphoto and Getty Images have tons of great pictures—for a price. If you work for a big company, they might have a contract with one of these services or have their own bank of licensed images for you to use.

If you're on your own, stock photos can cost anywhere from $10 to more than $100 each. Even if you get a bulk discount, the charges will add up fast.

Find Free Images

Luckily, there are lots of high-quality photos and images available for free. My favorite source is stock.xchng, but I've also used Compfight and Flickr Creative Commons.

The pictures on these sites are taken and posted by people of varying skill levels—usually amateurs. Some are very good and others look like your typical snapshots. But all are available royalty-free.

The restrictions on usage vary from artist to artist. Some pictures are for noncommercial purposes only. Some photographers require permission in advance, and others just want to be notified. Most expect credit, which you can accomplish in a slide at the end of the deck.

You might have to wade through a lot of poor-quality images that are not quite relevant, but the search engines on these sites are pretty good, and most of the photos are tagged or arranged in categories (people, sports, nature, etc.).

Get Creative

Some images are easy to locate, especially if your concept is simple and concrete. If you're talking about workplace stuff, you can find countless pictures of people meeting in conference rooms.

If your concept is time, there are tons of fancy clock faces. If you want to represent a challenge, you'll come across lots of mountain-climbing photos.

But some concepts require more creative thinking. For one of my presentations, I needed to illustrate the idea of confronting unpleasant tasks, which is a little abstract. After some thought, I searched through photos of piles of laundry and stacks of dirty dishes. I ended up using a simple picture of a stalk of broccoli.

For a slide on how stories humanize you, I found a picture of bare feet standing on a beach. For service, I came up with a hotel desk bell.

So be prepared to stretch your imagination as you search.

DIY

Probably the most hassle-free source of images is you. So scour your family albums and vacation photos.

Or commission your own. Need to illustrate the concept of "challenge"? Take a picture of your kid climbing a tree, or snap pictures of runners at a local 5K race.

I find myself taking all kinds of photos around town on my iPhone—street signs, bare trees, open windows—anything that I think might come in handy later.

Other Ways to Be Visual

Beyond pictures, here are a few other ways to add visual appeal and variety to your presentation:

- Video can be very powerful. It's especially effective for bringing in outside perspectives—the voice of the customer, employee, or investor, for instance.

- Your imagery doesn't have to be confined to just two dimensions. Remember show and tell? Try using a prop or two.

- There's no reason why your charts and graphs have to be ugly. If you find yourself having to interpret your chart for your audience, it's too complicated. Get rid of all those data points and show trends instead. Put the data in a leave-behind document.

PowerPoint Doesn't Suck. You Do.

That's the headline on an excellent blog post by digital marketing expert and professional speaker Mitch Joel. He's another advocate for dumping the templates and creating beautiful, image-heavy presentations from scratch.

Mitch mentions that he's often asked for a copy of his slide deck. But because he designs it as visual support, the deck alone would make no sense to people who didn't attend his talk:

> I would argue that the best presentations in the world are the ones where the slides are completely meaningless unless you have seen the speaker present them. Focus on that. Ensure that your slides act as a visual enhancement to everything

that you're saying. Why? Because if they don't, it means that there was never a need to have the presenters there in the first place, because everything was self-evident from the words on the slides.

For a free primer on creating presentations from scratch, check out the excellent tutorial from Design Shack referenced below.

A Smart Investment

Creating presentations that break free of the copy-dense, bullet-point-laden PowerPoint convention isn't easy, of course. It'll take time and effort.

But if it's something you'll be using over and over, the investment will be worth it. And believe me, your audiences will thank you.

Resources

- "7 Lessons from the World's Most Captivating Presenters," by Marta Kagan, *Hubspot*

- "Really Bad PowerPoint," by Seth Godin, *Seth's Blog*

- "PowerPoint Doesn't Suck. You Do," by Mitch Joel, *Six Pixels of Separation*

- "10 Tips for Designing Presentations That Don't Suck," by Joshua Johnson, *Design Shack*

SIN #7:
LOW-ENERGY DELIVERY

"I am the decisive element. It is my personal approach that creates the climate. It is my daily mood that makes the weather. I possess tremendous power to make life miserable or joyous. I can be a tool of torture or an instrument of inspiration."
Johann Wolfgang von Goethe, writer

When I was a student at Second City's training center, I was cast in my very first stage show. I had no idea what I was doing—and believe me, it showed.

Which way is upstage and which is down? What does "cheat out" mean? How do I project my voice?

But the biggest mystery to me was the concept of energy. I'll never forget those early rehearsals—the director kept yelling, "Rob, keep your energy up!" and "More energy!" and finally just "ENERGY!!"

I've since learned what energy is. It's subtle and complex, combining both the mental and the physical spheres. It requires both emotional and intellectual focus.

And it means you have to concentrate on what you are saying while at the same time remaining intensely aware of what's going on around you.

Energy can truly make or break your presentation. If your energy is flat, it's like sending your audience to a dull kind of purgatory.

So here are some things you can do to deliver an energetic performance.

Warm Up

Before going onstage, take a few moments to get focused. If you can, separate yourself from others.

Do some stretches and some deep breathing to get physically in the game.

Mentally, clear your head of the day's distractions. Walk through your presentation outline in your mind or practice the introduction. Do whatever affirmations work for you to psych yourself up.

Turn Up the Volume

If you remember nothing else, remember this: volume, volume, volume. *Speak up!*

People shouldn't have to strain their ears and lean forward in their seats to figure out what you're saying. Eventually they will tire of the struggle and just give up.

How loud should you speak? Louder than an intimate conversation you'd have over coffee with a close friend. Loud enough for them to hear you in the back row. Not "cheesy, old-school announcer" loud—it should be your natural voice, but at an elevated level.

Even if you're speaking through a microphone, you'll want to invest your words with a little more ... oomph. (That would be the passion and conviction I talk about later.)

So if you're a naturally quiet person, you have to learn how to overcome that. It may be unfair, but soft-spokenness can be interpreted as meekness or lack of confidence. Try an acting class or vocal lessons. They'll teach you techniques to help you speak from your diaphragm and project your voice.

Otherwise, try practicing around the house. Enlist a friend, family member, or colleague to keep you honest. Give him or her permission to let you know when your voice is trailing off.

Not only will a little extra volume create the appearance of an energetic performance, but the act of speaking up will actually give you an energy boost.

Stand Up, Sit Up

Of course, the default position when speaking to large groups is to stand. When you're in front of smaller groups, as in a conference room, the protocol's trickier.

If it's just six people, standing might appear a little weird. In a group of 20, it's probably a good idea. You'll have to use your judgment. Just keep in mind that standing will give your performance more energy.

And don't slouch. Stand up straight. That not only helps you to produce the volume you need but also projects confidence.

If you're seated, don't slump back in your chair. Sit up and lean forward, elbows on the table.

If you're part of a panel discussion, that can be tough in terms of energy. The usual setup has everyone seated behind a table, creating a physical barrier between the speakers and the audience. I think that's one reason panels are so often lifeless and boring.

Try lobbying the organizer or the group to ditch the table and use stools instead of chairs. If you absolutely have to sit, stay perched on the edge of your seat.

Bring the Passion

Speak with enthusiasm and conviction. If you're not excited about what you're saying, how do you expect your audience to get excited?

Years ago, comedian Ricky Gervais had an idea for a TV sitcom that was pretty radical for its time. It would be shot in "reality show style," with shaky handheld cameras, interviews that broke "the fourth wall," and a central character who was an insufferable jackass.

Gervais and his writing partner pitched their idea to the BBC, and the rest is history. "The Office" went on to become one of the most popular shows on British and American television.

How did such a crazy idea for a show get the green light? According to a BBC executive, it was the passion that the comic duo brought to their presentation:

> In their heads it was already a hit in Britain and a

hit in the U.S., and they were absolutely certain about it. And that sort of thing is infectious, and you think, Well, hooray—if they believe it, then I'll believe it. And maybe the actors will believe it, and maybe the viewers will believe it eventually. ("Ricky Gervais Would Like to Nonapologize," *New York Times Magazine*)

This is the kind of energy and passion you need to bring to your speech—a contagious enthusiasm that's irresistible to audiences. A sense of conviction and purpose that will make them believe in you and your ideas.

Speak with Intention

Invest every word and idea with meaning and intention. It's all too easy to go on autopilot, especially with material you're really familiar with. So stay connected at all times.

If you're describing a process, visualize the steps in your head. If you're talking about a person, picture his or her face. If you're discussing an idea, paint a mental picture. In other words, try to *experience* the things you're saying *as you say them*.

Maintaining this level of focus isn't easy, but it will keep you engaged and lend energy to your performance. It's what actors do, and it's why certain roles can be so demanding.

Be Here Now

Devote your full attention to being present and in the moment. If you're distracted or phoning it in, your audience will recognize it before you do.

So put your to-do list out of your mind. Stop thinking about the emails and voicemails piling up. Don't try to solve tomorrow's problem; focus on the one in front of you.

Turn off your internal editor—that nagging voice in your head that second-guesses your every move, punishes you for word flubs, and generally heckles your performance. Stay positive and keep moving forward.

At the same time, keep your senses on heightened alert. Be aware of what's going on around you. Tune in to your audience's mood and energy, and feed off of that to boost your own energy.

Don't Blame the Audience

Theater actors sometimes complain about a "bad" audience. They blame the crowd when jokes fall flat or certain moments don't land. They talk about a "weird energy" in the room.

The fact is, energy is a mysterious phenomenon. Some of it is within your ability to control and some of it is not.

So if people are quiet and sitting on their hands, it may be the culture of the organization, it may be the time of day, it may be what came before you or what's coming next. Maybe breakfast was bad or the coffee ran out.

Just do the things that are within your control to turn the situation around, and if it doesn't happen, don't blame the audience or yourself.

Unless, of course, this is something that happens consistently with your presentations. Then you might want to do some serious self-analysis.

Most of All, Be Sincere

Of course, I hope it goes without saying that you should bring enthusiasm and energy to your performance *because you are truly enthusiastic and passionate about the subject matter.*

If you tried to fake it, that would be the worst kind of sin (and you'd better be a damned fine actor). If you're not feeling passionate, you probably shouldn't be up there talking in the first place.

(And keep in mind that it's okay to turn down a speaking opportunity if you don't feel you can do it justice.)

Whatever you do, don't go into the dreaded cheerleader mode I talked about in the second chapter—"I am so PSYCHED about this topic! Who else is psyched? Come on, let's hear it, people!!!"

If you're not that type of person and if you don't have that kind of relationship with the audience, pushing the energy this way will probably fail.

Instead, let it come from within. Be focused, mentally and emotionally. Be present. Commit fully. Speak from the heart.

Remember, if you're checked out, your audience will quickly tune out.

SIN #8:
NO AUDIENCE INTERACTION

*"If you give an audience a chance,
they will do half your acting for you."*
William Hazlitt, writer

Most audiences today expect a certain level of interaction. So resist the temptation to lecture.

After all, part of what makes the presentation format unique among the various forms of communication is the opportunity for real face-to-face dialogue.

Interaction is about more than just setting aside time for Q&A (which you should definitely do). Think of it as leading a discussion as opposed to just delivering a speech.

Here are some tips on how to get your audience involved and make them a partner in the story you're telling.

Allow Time for Q&A

If you're filling a one-hour block of time, set aside at least 15 or 20 minutes for Q&A. Allow a similar percentage of time for shorter presentations.

If the organizers aren't planning time for Q&A, ask why not. With larger audiences, it may be difficult to pull off logistically. As a fair substitute, you could ask them to solicit and gather up written questions ahead of time.

Other than that, I see few good reasons not to take questions.

You can reserve time at the end of your presentation, or you can intersperse questions throughout. Many experts recommend that you not end with Q&A because of the risk of being taken off message or being derailed by some crank.

As speaking coach Michelle Mazur puts it:

> The conclusion of your presentation is what your audience members remember most. This is called "The Recency Effect." The conclusion needs to be memorable. Leave them with a message that sticks.

So you might want to take questions before your conclusion or have a brief summary prepared to wrap things up once the Q&A is done.

Don't Let Fear Get in the Way

A common concern people have is, "What if they ask a question I can't answer?"

To which I respond, "Get over it!" This is what leaders do.

Yes, Q&A can be tricky. But don't let that stop you from taking questions. Here are a few trouble spots and how to navigate them:

- If it's a question you don't know the answer to, simply say, "I don't know, but I'll get back to you." (Then make sure you do.) Nobody is expected to know everything—and if you set that expectation for yourself, be prepared for a lifetime of frustration and disappointment.

- If it's a really complicated question or one that's not relevant to most of the audience, offer to speak with that person afterward.

- If it's a sensitive issue that you're unable to address at this time, say so *and* explain why. Most people will accept "I can't discuss that" for an answer *if* you give them a little context, such as, "Personnel matters are confidential. If you were involved in a job action, you wouldn't want us talking publicly about it." Or, "This is the subject of pending litigation—anything I say here could harm our chances for success."

So don't let these worries keep you from engaging with your audience.

Be Ready to Kick Things Off

Sometimes you get an audience that is excited and gregarious and eager to jump in with questions. Other times, getting people to speak up is like raising the dead.

So you might have to prompt them a little. I have had spectacularly bad luck kicking off Q&A time with the generic, open-ended, "So ... any questions?" That's a little too abstract for some people.

It's better to get specific, as in:

- "I talked earlier about the power of emotion. Does anybody have an example of how you've used emotion to convince someone?"

- "What's your biggest frustration with PowerPoint?"

- "Some speakers wait until the end of their presentation to take questions, and others take questions throughout. Which do you prefer? Why?"

Once you get things rolling and people feel they have "permission" to speak up, you should be able to lead a productive conversation.

A Few More Tips

It's the nature of Q&A that your "true self" will be revealed—the one who's a little less guarded, less polished, more informal. That's to be expected. But there shouldn't be a stunning contrast between your "presenter persona" and who you are when answering questions off the cuff.

That means that your delivery, your tone, your demeanor, and the language you use should be authentic and true throughout your presentation, in both the scripted and unscripted moments.

A few other tips to keep in mind:

- If the audience members don't have access to a microphone, repeat or rephrase the question to make sure that others hear it (and to ensure that you understand what's being asked).

- A lot of speakers get into the habit of saying, "That's a great question!" every time they're asked something. If it truly is a great question, it's fine to say so, but this loses its impact when you say it over and over.

- When answering a question, try to bring things back around to your main points or messages.

- If you get stumped, try turning things back over to the audience: "I haven't come across this personally. Has anyone else had this issue, and would you like to talk about how you addressed it?" They will be floored by your lack of ego.

Carry On a Dialogue

You don't have to wait for a formal Q&A period to get your audience engaged. I use opportunities throughout my presentations to get people involved by encouraging them to complete my thoughts.

For instance, I might say:

- "It's important, of course, to know your audience. What are some things you would want to know about them before stepping onstage?"

- "Words are just one way to get your point across. What are some others?"

- "What is it about stories that makes them so powerful?"

I get really positive feedback when I conduct a presentation this way. The audience members feel they're a part of the conversation. And that makes it much more likely that they'll stay awake and alert.

Lead Exercises

Getting people up on their feet with exercises and group participation is another smart way to keep your audience engaged.

Here are some of the tactics I use and ways you can adapt them:

- As I mentioned earlier, I ask the audience to think about a great speech they've seen and to call out the qualities that made it special. Together we create a list on a flipchart or whiteboard. Think about asking your audience to describe their feelings, positive or negative, about the issue or problem you're addressing.

- I bring people up to perform scenes from a movie to illustrate storytelling, or I have them role-play some of the lessons I teach about energy and body language. Think about how you can get your audience involved, perhaps by coaching them through a scenario related to the points you're making.

- I do quizzes and trivia questions (related to my material, of course). "Who can tell me the first major film made from a David Mamet play?" "How many hours would you guess experts recommend you rehearse a speech?" Of course, it helps that I also give away prizes to the winners: books and candy.

Many speakers do big group exercises designed to get people's energy flowing or to get them moving around the room and meeting each other. That can be effective in the right hands. Or it can backfire if you're asking people to do something they're uncomfortable doing.

With all of these suggestions, it's important that you know your audience, or at least establish some trust and goodwill before you try something crazy, like enlisting them in a group chicken dance.

Share the Stage

Another effective tactic is to call on audience members to contribute their perspectives: "I was talking at the break with Karen from Utica about pricing issues, and she had a great idea. Karen, can you share that with the group?"

Obviously, you want to arrange things in advance so that there are no surprises, and you want to make sure your guests are poised and confident and can express themselves succinctly.

You don't have to bring them all the way up onstage—work with the production crew to get microphones and lighting into the audience at key points.

Now this obviously introduces more variables and risk to your presentation. What if someone you call on is out of the room? What if he or she runs on too long? What if the microphones don't work? But those issues can be mitigated with a little forethought and contingency planning.

And the payoff can be worth it. It breaks things up, adds variety, shows you're interested in the audience's perspective, and offers reinforcement of your message from someone the audience considers a peer.

It's Not About You

Okay, it really *is* about you. You're the one who's been invited to speak. You're the one people have to come to see.

But by encouraging discussion and participation, you also make it about them. And when it comes down to it, that's what most people are interested in.

Resources

- "How to Ruin a Presentation in the Last 30 Seconds," by Michelle Mazur, *Dr. Michelle Mazur*

SIN #9:
BUYING INTO BODY LANGUAGE MYTHS

"What you do speaks so loudly that I cannot hear what you say."
Ralph Waldo Emerson, writer

You've probably heard that "93 percent of all communication is nonverbal." Like a lot of conventional wisdom, that advice is flat-out wrong. It's a myth built on a misinterpretation of an isolated study that was done 40 years ago.

That study involved a group of subjects listening to a series of single words being spoken in either positive or negative tones. Its application to interpersonal communications has been widely debunked.

Even the study's author, Albert Mehrabian, has sought to clarify the record:

> I am obviously uncomfortable about misquotes of my work. From the very beginning I have tried to give people the correct limitations of my findings. Unfortunately the field of self-styled "corporate image consultants" or "leadership consultants" has numerous practitioners with very little psychological expertise.

Yet people continue to worship at the altar of the 93 percent theory.

Content Matters

Now, is body language important? Absolutely. Does it account for 93 percent of what you communicate? Who knows? The point is, it doesn't even really matter. It's a distraction from the real issue, which is intention (more on that in a moment).

To me, the biggest danger of the 93 percent figure is that it leads people to the misguided conclusion that their content barely matters, just so long as they give the audience a little razzle-dazzle and maybe some jazz hands.

Nothing could be further from the truth. Content and delivery go hand-in-hand, and determining which is more important is a pointless exercise.

Up in Arms over Body Language

Among the popular myths surrounding body language is the idea that you should never, ever cross your arms.

When I ask audiences what crossed arms signifies, they inevitably tell me it means you're defensive, closed off, stubborn. So I do an exercise where I cross my arms and talk for a moment. And then I ask, "Do I seem defensive, closed off, or stubborn?" They say no.

"But how can that be? I've got my arms crossed!" And they say it's because I'm smiling and I'm speaking in a warm, upbeat tone and making friendly eye contact.

And that's the whole point. We're not dummies. We don't judge random gestures in isolation—we look at the big picture.

So don't get yourself worked up over what to do with your arms or whether you should or should not put your hands in your pockets.

Concern yourself instead with your intention.

Focus Your Mind, and Your Body Will Follow

Focus your energy on being confident, warm, and positive, and the body language will flow naturally from that. Communication expert Nick Morgan puts it this way:

> [I]f you're going to give a speech, decide beforehand that you're thrilled to have the opportunity to present to this great group of people ... think first about what the purpose of the interaction is, what you want to get out of it, and what your attitude toward it is. If you focus your emotions in this way, your gestures will take care of themselves.

So gesture freely and naturally, as you would when talking with friends about something you're passionate about and really believe in.

And if you happen to cross your arms occasionally or even put your hand in your pocket? That's fine, as long as your attitude is good and you don't stick too long with any one gesture.

So Body Language Doesn't Matter?

That is not what I said. There are definitely some physical issues that will affect your performance for good or bad.

Plant Your Feet

The night before my wedding, we were at the rehearsal, and I guess I was nervous. (Something about all that "Do you solemnly vow before God and all these witnesses..." stuff.)

Without even being aware of it, I was shifting my weight back and forth from foot to foot like an angst-filled teenager asking a girl to the prom. And I wasn't a kid, either—this was 2012!

When you take your place onstage or at the front of the room, *own that space.* Own it like it's yours, bought and paid for. Plant your feet firmly on the ground. It projects confidence and poise. Because, of course, you're also *feeling* confident and poised, right?

Move Deliberately

That's not to say you should never move. You should. But you should move with intention and purpose.

David Meerman Scott is a marketing strategist and public speaker who often finds inspiration in the stagecraft of rock stars. He admires the way Mick Jagger uses the entire stage, going from side to side and even out into the audience. He observes:

Most public speakers either stand in front of the podium, or if they venture out, just hang out near the center of the stage. Some go back and forth to the corners like a metronome. True professionals work the entire stage like a rock star.

So use the whole stage. Don't get stuck in just one spot. Find key moments, such as transitions, when crossing the stage offers a visual cue that you're changing the subject. Approach the audience when you're making a really important point.

You can work yourself into a frenzy trying to choreograph the whole thing, but I'd rather you focus, again, on the internal. And as you rehearse (which we'll soon talk about), take note of where your body wants to take you. Your natural instincts, *when they're grounded in confidence*, are probably right.

Make Eye Contact

Some speakers are nervous about looking audience members in the eye. They might focus instead on a point out in the distance.

That's a bad idea. If you're going to be speaking regularly, you need to get used to making eye contact with people.

And if you're doing a good job, those little points of connection can actually help you. As you absorb the meaningful looks and the affirming nods, you can convert those positive feelings into energy to fuel your performance.

So scan the room as you speak—side to side, front to back. Don't ignore the people in the cheap seats (or any of the seats). Pause for a few seconds on a friendly face and move on.

This is another subject that raises the "How much is too much?" question. Believe me, you will know when you're making too much eye contact because it will start to feel creepy—to you and to the person on the receiving end of your lingering gaze. A few seconds will do.

Read Your Audience

The true value of body language for public speakers comes in discerning what's going on in the minds of your audience members. Are they bored? Annoyed? Skeptical?

You should be able to figure that out by noting if they are restless, slouched back in their chairs, reluctant to return eye contact, chattering among themselves, yawning, frowning, furrowing their brows, leaving the room, throwing things at you, etc.

In fact, modern technology has blessed us with an easy-to-read signal of an audience's engagement: the smartphone. Whereas in days of yore, audience members would flip through their program or sneak a peek at a newspaper or just stare blankly into space, today they freely bury their faces in their cell phone screens.

There's always going to be some of that going on. (And some of those people might actually be live-tweeting your speech.)

But if most people are surfing and texting? Or if more and more people become immersed in their screens as your speech goes on? That's a sign that whatever you're doing isn't working.

Make a Change

So it's probably a good idea to shake things up. Here are a few things you can do to turn things around:

- Increase your energy.

- Quicken the pace.

- Skip to a different section of the speech.

- Ask a question.

- Take an informal survey.

- Start an exercise.

Whatever you do, don't just stick with your original game plan and hope for the best. As we all know, the definition of insanity is doing the same thing over and over and expecting a different result.

Bringing It All Together

As you can see, a lot of the lessons from this book are starting to come together. If you have the awareness and presence of mind we talk about in chapter 7 (on energy), you'll be better able to read the room.

And if you need to change things up, chapter 8 (on interaction) will help you get your audience engaged.

In terms of being prepared when things go off the rails, that's what our next chapter is all about.

Resources

- "Busting the Myth 93% of Communication Is Nonverbal," by Jeremy Dean, *PsyBlog*

- "Mehrabian and Nonverbal Communication," by Olivia Mitchell, *Speaking about Presenting*

- "Weird Jewelry or Brilliant Solution to an Age-Old Speaking Problem?" by Nick Morgan, *Public Words*

- "What Mick Jagger Teaches Us About Public Speaking," by David Meerman Scott, *WebInkNow*

SIN #10:
INADEQUATE REHEARSAL

"All the real work is done in the rehearsal period."
Donald Pleasence, actor

Woe to the audience whose speaker decides to just wing it, for they shall be trapped in the pit of despair.

Improvisation may work in the hands of a true professional. (Then again, the professional almost always commits to preparation and practice.) But for most speakers, it results in a lot of meandering and missed opportunities.

Why do people think they can just get up there and perform on the fly? Maybe they overestimate their own abilities. Maybe it's bravado ("I did a Half-Ironman in under five hours—I got this!"). Maybe they just don't want to take the time.

But from what I've observed over the years, one of the biggest hang-ups that business presenters have about rehearsal is the concern that they'll appear "too scripted." They feel that if their performance is too smooth, they'll come across as slick, overproduced, inauthentic.

Take It from an Actor

I've actually found the opposite to be true. The more I plan and prepare, the more comfortable and spontaneous I'll appear.

Actors will easily spend over a hundred hours rehearsing for a stage show. They work their lines, practice their movements, think through all the relationships, explore all the nuances, try different things. And ultimately the result of all that preparation is freedom.

That's right—freedom. The script is no longer a straitjacket. It's so thoroughly embedded in their consciousness that it flows forth naturally. It's the difference between riding a wave and swimming against the tide.

Freeing yourself from the worries about what comes next and how something should be phrased allows you to live in the moment, play with the material, and—dare I say it—have fun.

So How Long Should You Rehearse?

I love to ask this question of audiences: "For a one-hour speech, how many hours of rehearsal do experts recommend?"

The guessing usually starts at five hours. And each time I call out "higher," people's eyes get wider. Ten? Fifteen? Twenty? When we finally land on 30 hours, they don't quite believe it.

But that's the recommendation of one of the foremost experts in the business, Nancy Duarte. Thirty hours to rehearse a one-hour speech. (And that doesn't include creating the content and the slides, by the way. Throw in another 60 hours for all that!)

Now, if you're in the unfortunate position of delivering several different PowerPoint presentations a week, you're not going to have that kind of time.

But if it's a really big speech—an important opportunity, such as an annual meeting for shareholders or employees or salespeople, or an address before a big industry or professional group—then you're going to want to invest some serious time rehearsing.

Here's some advice on how to prepare for your moment in the spotlight.

Anticipate Objections

Know your stuff. Know it backward, know it forward, know it sideways. Think of every hole in your argument, every possible objection, and be prepared to answer them—either in the presentation itself or in the Q&A.

Knowing your subject cold will boost your confidence immensely. In fact, I've found that the number-one cure for stage fright is mastery of your material.

Internalize, Don't Memorize

If you try to memorize your presentation word for word, you will come across as stilted. (Unless you're a good actor!)

And you're more likely to get tripped up as you grasp for the precise phrasing you've scripted.

It's better instead to "internalize." Break up your presentation into bite-sized chunks, one idea or point at a time. Get to know each one. Go over it in your head again and again. Don't worry about the specific words; just get the gist down.

Then start melding these chunks together, one section of the speech at a time. Practice it whenever you have down time—in the car, in the shower, at the gym.

You may never say it quite the same way twice, which is the whole point. When you've got the core of it internalized, you can deliver it with confidence while still leaving room to play around the edges—ultimately producing that feeling of an authentic, on-the-spot performance.

One important tip: your speech is going to be a lot easier to internalize if it's written in your own true voice—the way you speak in everyday conversation. If you're not comfortable with rhetorical flights of fancy, it's better to stay grounded.

Practice on Your Own—Out Loud

A speech is meant to be delivered aloud, so you absolutely must practice it out loud. Seriously. If you attempt to do it all in your head, sitting in front of your computer screen, you might as well not bother.

Get up on your feet and perform it as you would onstage. This will help you catch and unravel long-winded sentences and tongue twisters early on.

It's also the only way to get a true sense of how long the presentation is. And you definitely want to adhere to the time limits you've been given. Running over your allotted time is unforgivable.

In fact, you should plan to come in under the assigned time. No audience member ever left a speech saying, "Man, I wish that presentation had been longer!"

Finally, I find practicing aloud helps me identify weak spots. When I sense things are dragging and I get bored, I make cuts.

Practice in Front of Others

A speech is nothing without an audience, so it's a good idea to test your material in front of people beforehand. Ideally it should be work colleagues or industry peers—people who are knowledgeable about the subject matter and the target audience.

But if you trust friends or family members to give you honest, constructive feedback, that will work, too.

If you can, perform it a couple of times at different stages of development. And *really* perform it, just as you would onstage. Believe me, nobody wants to watch you halfheartedly phone it in. And that doesn't help your preparation either.

Take note of your audience's reactions. What seems to work? What doesn't? Are there places where you'll want to pause? Points you want to hit harder? Get their feedback.

Just be careful: if a certain line gets a big laugh or response with your test audience, don't assume it will happen at show time, too. No two audiences are alike, and pausing expectantly for a laugh that never comes is pretty awkward.

Videotape Yourself

The absolute best way to become aware of your tics and habits, both physical and verbal, is to watch yourself on video.

The camera does not lie. In fact, it can be downright brutal.

At the same time, understand that video can only approximate what actually happens in the room. It captures just two dimensions, so it can't convey the energy or chemistry of the moment or what the audience is doing.

So don't beat yourself up too much. You're probably not as bad as you think. Use video mainly as a tool for spotting technical issues with your performance.

Use Notes If You Need Them

At performance time, most people like to have notes in front of them. I think that's a fine idea. If nothing else, they offer a security blanket.

But keep the notes spare—bullet points as opposed to full sentences. It's very hard to dip in and out of verbatim notes that may or may not match up with the way you're phrasing things live. That disconnect can result in a verbal train wreck.

Also, keep the notes on cards, as opposed to big floppy pieces of paper.

Rehearse On-Site

Have you ever noticed how celebrities on awards shows manage to screw up the simple task of reading scripted babble and handing off trophies? And these are professional performers! What chance do the rest of us have to deliver a flawless performance?

Well, flawless is a high bar, but you can improve your odds of success by doing one thing those movie and TV stars likely failed to do: take the rehearsal process seriously.

If you're speaking at a big conference, there will probably be a full rehearsal the night or morning before your speech. Make the most of this opportunity. I've seen countless executives sabotage important speeches by squandering precious rehearsal time.

Here are a few things you can do to make things easier on yourself and others.

Be On Time

It's disrespectful and costly to keep a huge crew of people waiting for you. Plus, why alienate the people who have their fingers on the buttons that control your microphone, your lighting, and your visuals? You want them on your side, so don't be a diva.

Be Prepared

This should be one of your last rehearsals, not the first. If you're just now looking seriously at the script for the first time, you're in for a long night.

Stop Editing

At this point, you need to lock down your content. You can always come up with a better idea or another amusing anecdote or a different order, but messing with your script and slides the night before just introduces more opportunities for mishaps at performance time.

You may think it's just a handful of changes, but multiply that by the number of other speakers, and imagine the overworked, stressed-out crew members behind the scenes juggling a bunch of last-minute issues. It's a formula for disaster.

"Saturday Night Live" producer Lorne Michaels famously said, "We don't go on [the air] because we're ready; we go on because it's 11:30." Let go of the words and focus on your performance.

Listen

Put the phone away, stop the side conversations, and pay attention to what the producers are saying. Big events have many moving parts, and while you may be a big shot back at the office, here you're just another cog in a very large wheel.

Don't Phone It In

If you have the luxury of being able to run through your entire speech, make the most of that opportunity. Invest it with all the focus, energy, and volume you would devote to the actual performance. The more you work that muscle, the more easily you'll be able to "bring it" at show time.

Sometimes you'll get to rehearse only bits and pieces—transitions, audiovisual cues, etc. Make the most of this time anyway. Get a feel for the stage. Walk around. Figure out where the best light is. Learn how to advance your slides. Pause a moment and visualize what the place will be like full of people.

If It's Worth Doing, It's Worth Rehearsing

You may not get everything you want out of rehearsal. It's as much for the people producing the event as it is for you. But if you approach the process with the right mind-set, it's sure to pay off with a better performance—especially if you've done all the other planning and prep work before you arrive at the venue. Rehearsal really begins with you.

Resources

- "10 Ways to Prepare for a TED-format Talk," by Nancy Duarte, *Duarte*

SIN #11:
A WEAK FINISH

"Great is the art of beginning, but greater is the art of ending."
Lazarus Long, character in Robert Heinlein novels

Just as you should open strong, you should finish strong.

Of course, your middle should be strong, too. All of it should be strong.

There's no place for your B material. If you have weak parts, strengthen them. Or cut them. Make it all strong.

Fortunately, you can go a long way toward finishing strong simply by finishing—truly concluding things. When it comes to ending a speech, most people don't know where to begin. They just stop abruptly or trail off, leaving their audience in limbo.

What Not To Do

"In conclusion..."

"In closing..."

"I'd like to conclude by saying..."

"All in all…"

Those are examples of what not to do. I mean, they're perfectly serviceable, but they are ordinary. They're what's expected.

If you apply yourself, you can do better. Here are some tips on how to wrap things up in a way that's creative and interesting. And you don't have to choose just one—this is a mix-and-match menu.

Tell a Story

I like to finish with a story, for all the reasons I've discussed about the power of storytelling.

Of course, I make sure it reinforces the theme or messages I've already laid out or advances them to another level.

This is also an opportunity to get personal and reveal a little more of yourself. Master storyteller Nancy Duarte does this to great effect in one of her popular TED Talks.

Early on, she hints at the difficulty of her childhood, and in the end she lays herself bare. It has the impact of a roundhouse kick to the solar plexus.

Complete an Earlier Story

Another effective technique is to revisit a story you told earlier and add an extra bit of information—something you left out, a surprising twist, someone else's perspective, an epilogue or postscript.

Think of it as cashing in on the emotional investment the audience has already made in your story. It's easier to grow something that's established than to create something new.

Reinforce Your Key Points

This is from the old playbook of "Tell them what you're going to say, say it, and then tell them what you just said."

It's not going to dazzle anybody, but it can be effective, either on its own or in combination with a well-told story. If you're going to do it, you might as well be explicit about it:

- "If there's one thing I want you to remember, it's this…"

- "The three things to keep in mind are…"

- "What I hope you take away from all this is…"

Deliver a Call to Action

What do you want them to do? Buy your product? Hire your company? Make a contribution? Approve your idea? Implement your recommendations? Invite you to the next round? Seek out more information? Think differently? Act differently?

This is not the time to be coy. Be explicit:

- "If you agree with me, here are three simple things you can do right now to make a difference…"

- "This just scratches the surface. We'd love to come back and show you more…"

- "All of this great work doesn't get done for free. We need your help. Here's how you can contribute..."

- "If you like what you've heard, there's a lot more in my book, which you can purchase here..."

The idea of asking or selling is anathema to a lot of people, but what makes it easier is building an irresistible case (through stories and emotion, especially) that makes your audience want to help.

Raise and Answer a Question

Try addressing your audience's biggest fear or objection:

- "You may think this is too hard/too expensive/too time consuming. Let me tell you why that's wrong..."

- "You may be wondering, 'Why now?' Here's why this is so urgent..."

- "You may say, 'We've tried this before.' Here's why it's different this time..."

Going back to the idea of knowing your audience, few things are more powerful than the feeling that you're reading their minds. So do your homework.

Paint a Picture of the Future

What does the world look like if your audience acts now? What if they fail to act? Offer that carrot or stick. Or both.

- "Imagine a world where..."

- "Picture yourself five years from now..."

- "Monday morning you're at your desk. You have two options..."

Offer Inspiration through Example

If you're asking your audience to do something difficult, offer them hope that it can be done:

- "I know we can do this because we've done it before. Ten years ago..."

- "Five years ago, our chief competitor was in a similar position. Look at them now..."

- "Jeff Bezos faced a similar crossroads with Amazon..."

So think about people and organizations your audience admires or cultural touchstones that resonate, and capitalize on those.

Exit, Stage Left

A few final things when you're all through:

Soak Up the Applause

I don't consider myself a particularly humble person who shies from the limelight, but I still feel funny accepting an audience's applause at the end. I have to restrain myself from looking down or immediately gathering up my things and disconnecting my laptop or dashing offstage.

If your audience is kind enough to show their appreciation, take the time to acknowledge it. Plant yourself, look people in the eye, say thank you, nod your head—maintain that final moment of connection before stepping down.

Resist Housekeeping Duties

Your conference organizers might ask you to do a little housekeeping when your speech is over, à la "Lunch will be served downstairs in the Riviera Room (escalators on the left as you exit), where you'll have your choice of chicken piccata or grilled halibut..."

If you get a request like this, ask if someone else can take care of it. Big events should have a designated emcee, from either the staff or the production crew, to take care of matters like these. If you do it, it will just diminish the power of your rousing conclusion.

Know Where to Go

You paid attention in rehearsal, right? Like I told you to do in the last chapter? Good. Then you should know how to get off the stage.

Sometimes it will be obvious. But if you're not prepared, you might find yourself bumping into the next presenter, running over a member of the wait staff, or getting lost in a maze backstage. So make sure you have an exit plan.

Stick Around

People will usually want to come up and talk to you afterward. They might want to tell you how much they loved your talk, share a story from their own experience, ask you a question, or hand you their card.

Be open to that. It's all part of the gig. Expect to hang around for 15 or 20 minutes.

Thank the Organizers ... but Not Too Much

Whoever helped make this happen should be acknowledged and thanked personally. Of course, they should thank you, too, so it'll likely be a great big love fest.

I've seen speakers reel off a long list of thank-yous in their speech, but I think that's a waste of time and a little pretentious—it's not like you're accepting an Oscar.

Thank the person who introduced you or acknowledge someone in the audience you're particularly close to, but dispense with the laundry lists.

The Afterworld

Of course, the end of your speech is just the beginning of the next one. After the applause dies down but before you move on to your next priority, take stock.

What worked and what didn't? Were there any surprises? Anything you need to add to your pre-speech routine or checklist next time?

Did an issue come up in the Q&A that you need to brush up on? Or did it suggest content you might want to add to the body of your speech?

At some events, audience members fill out evaluation forms. Make sure you get those results when they're available and see what you can learn from them—along with any informal feedback you heard from audience members.

And if you're fairly new to this, take a moment to celebrate a little. Getting up in front of people and sharing your ideas is a courageous thing, so pat yourself on the back. You earned it.

Resources

- "The Secret Structure of Great Talks," by Nancy Duarte, *TED.com*

CONCLUSION:
ARE WE REDEEMED YET?

The sins of public speakers and presenters are many, and narrowing them down to 11 has been a tough task. In fact, these probably should be called the 11 deadli*est* sins—the worst of the worst.

They also happen to be the kind that are within the average person's ability to control. You don't have to be a master presenter to overcome them.

But this is by no means an exhaustive list. Here are a few other sins you'll want to avoid.

Inauthenticity

Being fake is definitely a deadly sin, and I could have made it one of the 11, but I feel that authenticity is a natural byproduct of avoiding many of the other sins.

If you create a genuine connection with your audience, if you tell stories that are meaningful to you, if you speak from the heart and with conviction and put real passion behind your words, that will all contribute to an authentic performance.

I've worked with speakers who worry that they don't have enough "stage presence" and feel they have to be someone else in front of an audience. Nonsense. I've seen plenty of speakers who register low on the charisma meter but still manage to move the needle with audiences through their sincerity, the depth of their knowledge, and the quality of their ideas.

So please don't feel you have to add a bunch of razzle-dazzle or use formal, soaring rhetoric if that rings false to you. (And definitely ignore the advice I once got that you shouldn't use contractions in a speech!)

Remember: it's a conversation. Be yourself. Albeit a slightly heightened, more energetic, more focused version of yourself.

Flat, Monotone Delivery

To keep your audience engaged, you should do your best to modulate your volume and pacing. Get a little louder at the passionate parts, and bring it down occasionally for dramatic effect.

And vary your speed. You might want to accelerate as you build to the climax of a story, but be sure to tap on the brakes at key points as well.

Speaker coach Barbara Kite says that 95 percent of her clients speak too fast. It's a common problem, especially when we're nervous. But people need time to absorb what you're saying. So take it easy, and go back to the advice about putting intention behind every word.

Failure to Recover from Flubs

You will make mistakes. You'll mispronounce a word, skip a slide, bump the microphone. This stuff happens, and no amount of preparation is going to guarantee a flawless performance. There are just too many factors beyond your control.

What you can control, though, is your reaction to these events. In acting, there's a concept called continuity of intent. It means that no matter what happens, you don't break character.

So keep calm and carry on. The more you call attention to your mistakes, the more your audience will notice and remember them. Don't apologize or explain or wince—just keep going.

I've suffered equipment breakdowns, I've skipped whole sections of my speech, I've had the wrong version of my slides loaded. But few noticed because I didn't make a big deal out of it.

No Soundbites

Remember, some of those audience members buried in their phones and tablets are actually sharing bits of your presentation on social media. So be sure to give them some material to work with.

Simplify your best ideas into short soundbites. They don't have to be catchy slogans, just succinct and meaningful.

One point that people frequently tweet from my presentations is, "Treat every communication like a performance." That's not poetry or anything, but it's short and straightforward.

Marketing CEO Gini Dietrich talks about her "chili con queso" test. If she doesn't come away with some flavorful content to share, she considers the speech a bust.

Lack of Humor

In movies and TV, even the most serious dramas offer comic relief once in a while. It breaks the tension and creates little surprises that delight audiences. So make use of humor where you can.

But don't try too hard to be funny. Look for those small moments of truth: the little details of life that resonate, the self-deprecating asides that humanize you, the inside jokes that help your audience connect to you.

Treating a Webinar Like a Regular Speech

Presenting online can be a surreal experience. It's like shouting into a dark well—only without the helpful feedback that the echo provides.

So you'll need to work even harder to keep your audience's attention on you and your material, as opposed to the dozen browser tabs they have open on their desktop.

That means boosting your energy level even further, quickening the pace, creating more powerful visuals, and making the most of whatever interactive tools are available—polls, quizzes, chat windows, etc.

Succumbing to Stage Fright

I believe that stage fright is part mental and part physical. On the mental side, take the steps outlined in chapter 10 (rehearsal) to ensure that you are as prepared as possible. The more confident you are in your material, the more assured you will be onstage.

On the physical side, take care of yourself. Get enough sleep, eat right, reduce distractions, do some pre-show warm-ups like stretching, and, most of all, be sure to breathe.

And keep reminding yourself that you belong there, that you have really valuable insights to share, and that your audience is pulling for you to inform and entertain them.

Go Forth and Sin No More

As I said in the opening to this book, most people are not very good presenters. And that offers a great opportunity for you to stand out.

No, not everyone is going to reach the ranks of the Speaker Hall of Fame (yes, that's an actual thing). But I do believe that anyone can get better. More confident, more comfortable, more engaging.

Work on a few of these tips at a time. Learn from your mistakes and measure your progress against yourself.

Don't despair when you see a TED Talk that knocks it out of the park. That's not a fair comparison. Nobody who watches Tiger Woods on TV expects to get off the couch and join the PGA Tour.

And don't let your subject matter limit your creativity. Just because you're not solving world hunger or unveiling the new iPad doesn't mean you can't dress up a presentation on, say, wastewater treatment strategies with story and visuals.

Remember, enthusiasm is contagious, and passion can make up for a multitude of sins. Put all your energy and heart into it, and your audience will be on your side.

Resources

- "A Surefire Way to a Memorable Speech," by Barbara Kite, *blog*

- "Six Tips for Better Public Speaking," by Gini Dietrich, *Spin Sucks*

ACKNOWLEDGMENTS

I am grateful to all the outstanding speakers who have inspired me over the years. I'm also thankful for the bad speakers—they motivate me to help make the world's conference rooms and boardrooms a safer place for audiences.

It took a small village to produce this book. Derek Murphy at Creativindie designed the cover and Jane Dixon-Smith of JD Smith-Design did the interior. Elissa Rabellino of StyleInSites provided copyediting services and Liz Broomfield at LibroEditing did the final proofing. Pam Tierney engineered the audiobook. I am very grateful for their talent, skills—*and patience!*

Finally, many thanks to Karen, who patiently put up with me throughout this process.

ABOUT THE AUTHOR

Rob Biesenbach is a corporate communications pro, actor, and author. He's written hundreds of speeches for CEOs and other executives and is a professional speaker himself.

Rob is a former VP at Ogilvy PR and press secretary to a state attorney general, among other things. A Second City–trained actor and improviser, he has appeared in more than 150 stage and commercial productions.

Rob brings these two worlds together in his presentations and workshops, helping people communicate more successfully in the workplace, the marketplace, and their everyday lives.

ALSO BY ROB BIESENBACH:
ACT LIKE YOU
MEAN BUSINESS

Rob is the author of *Act Like You Mean Business: Essential Communication Lessons from Stage and Screen*. The book applies the best lessons from the world of movies, TV, and theater to help people communicate more effectively.

Readers learn how to better connect with audiences, tell more compelling stories, express ideas visually, and break through the obstacles to clear, effective communication. These are skills critical to winning business, driving sales, building customer trust, motivating employee performance, and inspiring teams.

Act Like You Mean Business was published in 2011 by Brigantine Media.

JOIN NOW

If you enjoyed this book, I invite you to join my email list. You'll get practical tips and the best thinking from experts to help you communicate more confidently and successfully.

For more information, visit RobBiesenbach.com.

Made in the
USA
Monee, IL